Incident at the Panama Canal

A Fuerte Life Adventure

Written by Giselle Fuerte
Illustrated by Pasurip

Copyright © 2020 by Giselle Fuerte
All rights reserved. No part of this book may be reproduced or used in any manner without written permission of the copyright owner except for the use of quotations in a book review.

First edition December 2020

ISBN 978-0-578-80821-5 (paperback)

Published by Real Life Bricks
www.reallifebricks.com

- The Fuerte Family (from left to right): Joey (Dad), Mosi, Arén, Serena (Mom), Jahi
- Arén and Jahi are twins.
- Serena was born in Panama City, Panama and is AfroPanamanian. Joey was born in California and is white American.
- The family lives in the mountain town of Boquete (Boh-keh-teh) in Panama.
- Spanish and English are widely spoken in Panama. The Fuerte Family is bilingual.

Table of Contents

CHAPTER 1 — 8

CHAPTER 2 — 14

CHAPTER 3 — 20

CHAPTER 4 — 26

CHAPTER 5 — 32

CHAPTER 6 — 38

ABOUT ALFRED SPRINGER — 44

GLOSSARY — 48

For Further Reading — 50

OTHER WORKS BY THE AUTHOR — 51

FOLLOW US ON SOCIAL MEDIA — 52

Jahi spent all week building his remote control Construktor bricks train set and was ready to show it to his family.

Jahi's dad, Joey, was first to see it. "You built this all by yourself, hm?" said Joey with a wink, holding up one car of the train to admire.

"Uh huh," nodded Jahi with a proud smile. He tipped his train conductor hat and announced, "The Panama Canal Railway is ready to go!"

"Jahi, this is going to look great next to our Panama Canal Construktor display for Día de los Muertos. Let's get the track set up on the dining table and give the train a test spin," said Joey.

In the dining room, Jahi's mom, Serena, and his brothers, Mosi and Arén, gathered around the table to watch the installation of the new addition to the Día de los Muertos display to honor their ancestors.

Jahi and his dad set up the track around the canal so that it wrapped around

it in a loop. Jahi carefully laid each car of the train onto the track, making sure they all connected. He picked up his remote, ready to take the train for its first trip.

"Ready, everybody?" asked Jahi, looking around at his family with a smile.

"Let's give it a whirl, little dude!" Joey encouraged.

Jahi turned a knob on the controller, ready for the train to lurch forward and race around the track, but nothing happened... He turned the knob again, and still nothing happened.

"Is it going to go?" asked Mosi.

"Why isn't it working?" asked Arén.

"I don't know what's going on," said Jahi in frustration, taking off his train conductor hat and letting it fall to the floor.

"Well, let's not forget what your friends, Ada and Cece, often suggest: troubleshoot to figure out what's wrong," offered Mom.

"Hm," started Jahi, "Let me think. The batteries are new so that can't be the issue. But maybe…" Jahi trailed off as he ran back to his room and returned with his screwdriver.

He used the screwdriver to open the remote control's battery compartment and checked to make sure the batteries were in the correct position. He repeated the process by checking the battery pack in the train. When he was done, he said, "All of the batteries are in correctly."

"Oh! I know! I'll also make sure everything is connected the right way," he

said. He checked the connection points between the receiver and the battery pack, and then between the train motor and the receiver. Everything looked good.

"I don't understand what the problem

is," he said. He turned the knob a few more times and, when the train still wouldn't move, he bowed his head and slumped his

shoulders.

"Oh bub, I'm know you're disappointed. Can I offer you a hug?" asked dad.

Jahi nodded and then threw himself against his dad's legs, wrapping his arms around him. Joey held him tight.

"It's ok, Jahi. We'll get it working," Mosi chimed in, putting a hand on his little brother's shoulder, but Jahi still looked sad.

Serena planted a kiss on the top of Jahi's head of dark curls and said, "Jahi, you may remember that your great-grandfather, your bisabuelo, was a train conductor at the Panama Canal. Except there, they call them mules instead of

trains."

Jahi barely nodded.

Serena continued, "He'd sometimes have train trouble and had to figure out, right on the spot, how to solve those problems. Maybe we can take a break and talk about one of bisabuelo's train stories. Giving our brains a break from trying to solve our own problem and looking at how others solve theirs might be just what we need to get our creative juices flowing and help us come up with new ideas to fix your train."

Jahi nodded again and wiped his eyes with a sleeve. He followed his mom to the sofa where he climbed into her lap. His dad and brothers joined them on either side of the sofa.

Serena opened a scrapbook on the coffee table. It was filled with photos of

their ancestors. Jahi looked at a faded photo of his bisabuelo conducting a mule that was towing a giant ship behind it.

"Did I tell you about the time your

bisabuelo saved a ship from crashing into one side of the Miraflores Locks?" asked Serena.

Jahi gasped. "Noooo," he replied, drawing out the "o," his eyes suddenly big with excitement and curiosity. Mosi and Arén smiled broadly and bounced up and down with anticipation.

As his mom began to talk, Jahi focused on the photo of his bisabuelo and, suddenly, it was as if he was transported back to that time.

Chapter 4

ت

Canal Dreams

Jahi's bisabuelo, Alfred, conducted the mule along one set of tracks, while his friend, Miguel, conducted the mule along

the other track. Between them, floating in the locks, was a tall and mighty cargo ship, loaded down with shipping containers.

Alfred and Miguel slowly tugged the ship through the locks. The air smelled salty, and the sun, for a moment, hid

behind some light, fluffy clouds. The steel lines that connected the cargo ship to the mules trailed behind their locomotives. As the mules conducted the ships forward from the Pacific Ocean, so that they could cross the width of Panama and be released into the Atlantic Ocean, Alfred wondered what might be inside the containers aboard the ship. *Was it construction equipment from Vancouver, Canada destined for Greenland? California Redwood furniture headed to Portugal? Clothing made in Mexico making its way to England?*

Suddenly, Alfred heard a loud splosh, and he was jolted from his thoughts when he felt his train jerk suddenly. It was as if he'd been pulled in a direction that definitely wasn't forward. He quickly tried to get his bearings by first looking at his control panels to see if something had gone wrong with any of the locomotive's systems.

Just then, he heard a loud creaking noise from behind, followed by the voices of canal workers yelling. "¡Miren! ¡Cuidado!" *Look! Watch out!*

Alarms blared, and someone from the control room yelled frantic orders over the PA system, "¡Trabajadores a sus estaciones de trabajo!" *Workers to your work stations!*

Alfred turned his head left and right to look for the source of the trouble when,

behind him, he saw the ship he was tied to veering toward his wall of the locks. He froze as he watched the ship's bow bob toward his track. Any minute it would hit the wall and cause major damage.

Alfred snapped himself out of his frozen state to quickly shuffle through options in his head. He could continue to panic and watch the ship bash into the wall, or he could put his training and experience into action and try to stop a possible catastrophe.

He picked up his CB radio to talk to Miguel. "¡A toda velocidad!" *Full speed ahead!*

Miguel followed Alfred's instructions and shifted into high gear. His mule sped forward and the cables connected to the

ship went taut and tight. The ship groaned as it veered toward the wall of Miguel's track and away from Alfred. After Miguel had gotten a head start, Alfred shifted into top speed and looked back to see his cables

stretch tightly between his mule and the ship. This pulled the ship so that it was now safely centered in the Locks.

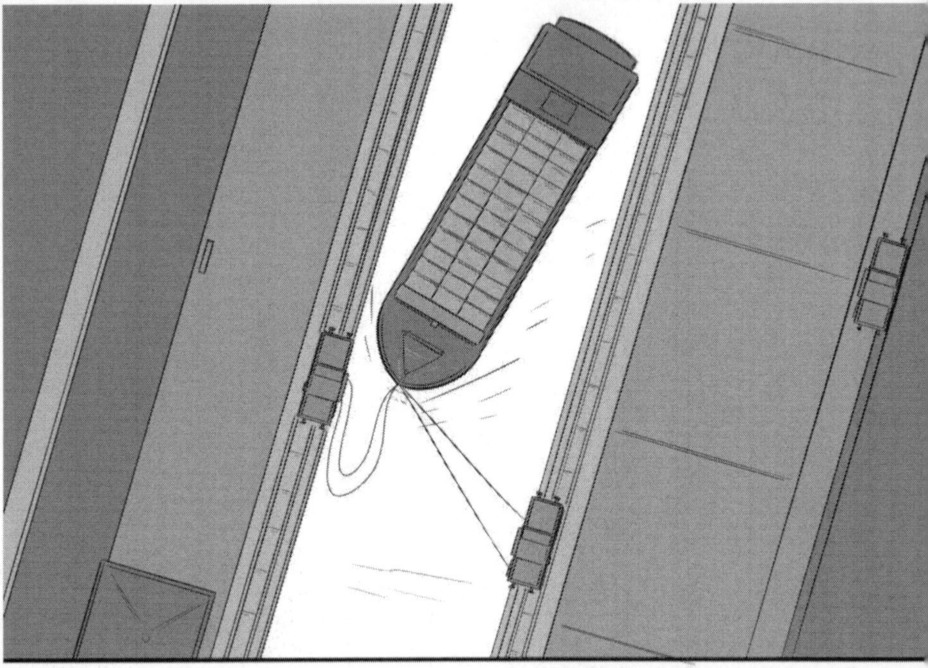

Canal workers all sighed in relief and the control room erupted in applause. "¡Bien hecho!" they cheered. *Well done!*

Chapter 6

دُ

All Aboard!

"Great-grandfather saved the day," said Jahi when his mom had finished telling the story.

"That's right, and he was scared and didn't know what to do at first. But he focused his mind and solved the problem," replied Serena.

"Never give up, right, mom?" asked Jahi with a smile.

"*Nunca te des por vencido*," Serena smiled back and leaned in to kiss Jahi on his forehead.

Jahi walked back over to his train set and the rest of the family followed. He picked up the remote and thought for a moment. "Hmm," he hummed to himself, and then, "hmm," again.

"I wonder if…" he began as he bent over to look more closely at the remote receiver installed in the train, and then at the remote in his hand. His face lit up as if a light bulb had gone on above his head, and he flipped a switch on the remote.

"Aha! The remote switch wasn't set to the same number as the selector switch on the receiver. Now, they match!" announced Jahi.

"Ah," nodded Jahi's dad, "I bet the Panama Canal Railway train is ready for its first trip now."

"Here we go," said Jahi, grimacing slightly as he prepared himself for disappointment. He pressed the remote trigger, and the train took off down and around the track, circling around and behind the Panama Canal display and back again.

Jahi and his family erupted in cheers. Mosi and Arén settled into a dining chair to watch the train go by.

"What a perfect way to remember our ancestors, Jahi!" said Serena.

About Alfred Springer

ALFRED SPRINGER (SECOND FROM LEFT)

Alfred Louis Springer was born in Panama on May 26, 1920. He worked as a tool dispatcher at the Miraflores Locks at the Panama Canal, and in the 1960s, he was chosen as the first Black Panamanian man to operate the locomotives/mules in the

Miraflores Locks — work, at that time, exclusively carried out by Americans.

ALFRED SPRINGER ON A MULE AT THE PANAMA CANAL

Alfred Springer is the author's grandfather and her children's bisabuelo. Although the author didn't get to know her

grandfather well when he was alive, she believes that his parents immigrated to Panama from Barbados to help build the Panama Canal. The story told in this book of saving the Locks from catastrophe is not a true account, though it is true that ships have crashed into the canal at one time or another.

Glossary

Día de los Muertos: A holiday where individuals and families gather to remember friends and family members who have died. The holiday originated and is primarily celebrated in Mexico, though it is also celebrated in many other countries in Latin America, including in Panama.

Miraflores Locks: Miraflores is the name of one of the three locks that form part of the Panama Canal.

Mules: Mules play an important role at the Panama Canal. They are tow locomotives that lead ships through the canal, and prevent them from hitting and damaging it.

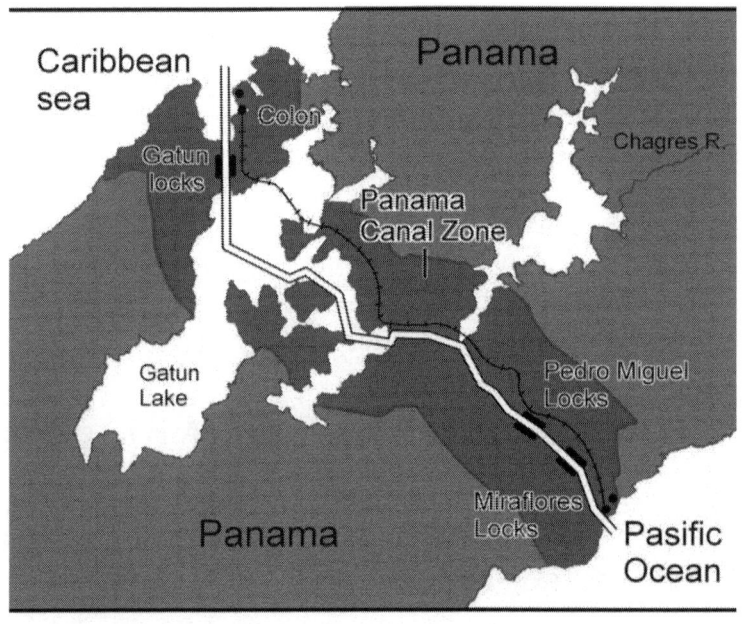

Panama Canal: The canal is a human-created waterway in the Latin American country of Panama. It connects the Atlantic Ocean with the Pacific Ocean. Although France and then the United States are credited with building the Canal, it was primarily workers from Barbados, China, India, Jamaica, and other countries who actually built the canal with their hands and labor. As a result of the building of the canal, Panama is one of the most ethnically, racially, and religiously diverse countries in Latin America.

Panama Canal Railway: A train rail line that links the Atlantic Ocean to the Pacific Ocean in Panama.

For Further Reading

- *Early Reader - The Panama Canal*, by Elbert Hoppenstedt
- *What Is the Panama Canal?*, by Janet B. Pascal and Who HQ

Other Works by the Author

Construction is So Fun!

The Lying Liar Called Racism: A Love Letter

Soccer Goals!: A Fuerte Life Adventure

Follow Us on Social Media
For New Releases

 facebook.com/reallifebricks

 instagram.com/playreallifebricks

 twitter.com/reallifebricks

Made in the USA
Middletown, DE
28 December 2020